# FOURTH GRADE NOTEBOOK

COMPOSITION JOURNAL
DOT GRID & WIDE RULED LINES
FOR NOTES & WRITING

## SUGGESTED USE:

TRY USING THE DOT GRID PAPER SECTION TO WRITE DOWN NOTES OR KEY IDEAS FROM LESSONS, OR USE IT FOR TAPING IN PARTS OF WORKSHEETS ETC, AND THE LINED AREA CAN BE USED FOR WRITING AND JOURNALING.

schoolnest

ART + BOOKS + NATURE



SECOND EDITION

WWW.THESCHOOLNEST.COM

# Thank You

## FOR PURCHASING A SCHOOLNEST NOTEBOOK

You can find a rainbow of notebook options in many school subjects (math, spelling, history timeline, science, grade level composition books, journals, and more) on: theschoolnest.com!

Follow along on instagram

**@SCHOOLNEST**

Made in the USA
Columbia, SC
18 July 2025